The Bullying Prevention Formula

BY:
MARC JOUAN

TABLE OF CONTENTS

CHAPTER 1:

HOW MARTIAL ARTS CAN HELP

Have you ever been bullied or do you know someone who has been the victim of bullying? Unfortunately, bullying is a very common problem, and recent statistics indicate its increasing prevalence. While adults may also be targets of bullying, data shows that the situation is worse among children and teenagers.

I'm Master Marc Jouan. For over twenty-five years, I've been teaching martial arts to children and adults of all ages. As an instructor at ATA Martial Arts in West Chester, Pennsylvania, I see children every day who suffer from low self-esteem and who have confidence issues looking to martial arts to help them through this difficult period in their lives. It is my firm belief that the martial arts can instill a sense of discipline and self-confidence that can carry over to all aspects of a young person's life.

When a child comes in for martial arts training, it's often because he or she is being bullied or there is a fear of becoming the target of bullying. Let's face it, bullying is widespread. Children see it happening, perhaps to a friend or a classmate.

How would they handle it if it happened to them?

Since bullies cannot exist without victims, how can a child, or anyone for that matter, avoid becoming a target? Typically, one should work on improving one or more of these four main areas:

1. Self-confidence
2. Physical fitness
3. Self-esteem
4. Self-defense skills

Of these four areas, we ask parents to choose which would be of greatest value to their child in our martial arts program, but in reality, it's a trick question. All four areas are interconnected, and it's hard to isolate and work on just one. Conversely, when you start to improve in one area, you will see improvement in the other areas as well. Improvement should be made in all four of these areas in order for kids to be able to stand up for themselves and thus become less of a target for bullying behavior.

I believe that martial arts helps to prepare people both physically and mentally. It gives them choices, and when people are armed with choices, they're more confident. That should be the mission of any good martial arts program, to provide empowerment while having fun.

CHAPTER 2:

SOME TRUTHS ABOUT BULLYING

Let's start with a quiz. This will help to illuminate some of the truths about bullying. People assume that they know certain things about bullies and bullying, when in fact, the opposite is often true.

Question 1

True or false: Those who bully others are insecure and have low self-esteem. They pick on others in order to feel better about themselves.

In response to this statement, most people will say "true." That's what they've often heard, and a lot of folks just make this assumption about bullies.

In fact, research shows that those who bully others have average or above-average self-esteem. They often have aggressive temperaments and a lack of empathy.

I was bullied when I was younger. The person who bullied me was a great athlete. He was a star football player and basketball player. He had a ton of friends, so he definitely wasn't picking on me to make himself feel better. He had plenty of other outlets for that , so whatever his reasons for being a bully, it certainly didn't have to do with his self-esteem. The fact that he had power and that he had people who would listen to him is what made him so dangerous.

People like this guy—star athletes, for example, and other "cool kids"—have a choice whether to do things the right way or the wrong way. Since they may serve as role models for others, these young people in particular have a responsibility to make correct choices. The boy who picked on me clearly made the wrong choice because he used his influence and power to make sure that others bullied me. It was for a silly reason, too—because I was not as good an athlete as he was. We'll talk later about the different types of bullies, and we'll recognize him as the "jock bully" who picks on others simply because they are not as gifted physically.

Question 2

True or false: Those who bully are looking for attention. If you just ignore them and the problem, the bullying will stop.

This answer is also false. People like to think that bullying will just stop, but research shows that those who bully are looking for control over others, and they rarely stop if their behavior is ignored. The bullying will continue unless it is brought to the attention of someone who can help course correct the situation.

Question 3

True or false: "Kids will be kids," and bullying is just a part of growing up.

Again, that is definitely false. Research shows that bullies seldom outgrow bullying. The bullying behavior is simply redirected. Sixty percent of boys identified as bullies in middle school committed at least one crime by the time they were 24 years old.

Let's go back to the boy who bullied me in seventh grade. I went to middle school with him, seventh and eighth grades. Later, we went to different high schools, so we lost contact, much to my delight. Some years later, it was brought to my attention that the boy who bullied me was in the newspaper. He had committed a misdemeanor crime, one that involved hostile behavior towards someone else, and was going to possibly serve some jail time. I wasn't the least bit surprised.

What you see over and over are people who have this type of temperament treating people a certain way. When they act out this behavior in school, their teachers, parents, or counselors should address it as soon as possible. Increasingly, this type of behavior, even at a young age, can result in sanctions ranging from school intervention via suspensions and/or expulsions to jail time for criminal misdemeanors and even felonies. Laws vary from state to state and new acts are being passed to help combat this ever-increasing threat. Imagine how having a criminal record for an act of bullying in school could change the rest of your life!

What if that same type of behavior occurs outside of school? If the behavior continues unchecked, it could lead to more severe forms of bullying or types of law-breaking. The law become involved and consequences get more harsh, not just a slap on the wrist or a day out of school. Often, these students require a support structure and a unified front from parents, teachers, school staff, mentors, and more to alter their behavior and to address any other challenges that may be influencing the bullying behavior.

Question 4

True or false: Kids can be cruel about differences.

This one is partly true. We know that kids can sense those who are different a mile away. But physical differences only play a small role in bullying situations. Most victims are chosen because they're sensitive, anxious, or unable to stand up for themselves.

In my school situation, I wasn't picked on because I looked different from the bully and his friends. I was bullied because I wasn't as good at playing sports as the other kids in our gym class. I wasn't able to play as well or keep up with the team, and that's what made me different and made me the target.

Question 5

True or false: Those who are tormented by bullies need to learn to stand up for themselves and deal with the situation.

Sometimes I see kids come to me who are looking for a quick fix to their bullying problem. But really, this statement is generally false. Those who are being bullied are usually younger or physically or emotionally weaker than those who are doing the bullying. The kids who are the targets may lack social skills, and they may not have friends who are able to defend them. They are less powerful and have a hard time defending themselves.

When kids come to me to learn martial arts, they're often looking for a quick cure. But what is that quick cure? Are we going to give you confidence in one class that you're going to be able to stand up to somebody? Confidence is built over time and with experience, repetition, comfort, and familiarity. Children are not going to gain confidence from something they learned in one martial arts class that they may not even remember when they leave the class. Even if they do remember, techniques and the confidence that goes with knowing them need to be reinforced and practiced over and over through training in all types of environments. We train techniques slowly, with repetition, and then under stress, with fatigue, and with other variables to ensure they can be done right. That's not going to happen overnight.

Are they looking for a physical solution? If they're looking for a physical technique to learn, and if that's how the kid is going to handle the situation, then he or she is going to get in as much trouble as the bully. Generally, hitting back in schools isn't the right answer unless you're prepared for the consequences that come with that. Don't get me wrong, in some instances, it can be a very appropriate action. Unfortunately, we live in a world where sometimes the child being bullied can face just as many disciplinary actions for his/her violent counterattack as the child who committed the bullying action in the first place. I believe that having the physical self-defense skills readily available should just be another tool in your toolbox. Of course, the level of countermeasures should also always be appropriate to what you're receiving.

Let's finish up the story of my bully and me. It all came to a head quickly when he got a few of his friends to surround me in the locker room to try and throw me into the showers with my clothes on. At this point, I had already been involved with martial arts training for several years, but it didn't prepare me for such a swiftly unfolding scenario. I felt one kid come up behind me and grab me in a bear hug as my bully stepped in front of me. I'm not sure what he was going to do, but I wasn't going to wait and find out. I managed to wriggle out of the other kid's grip, turned, and threw a punch that was enough to move him. It all caught him by surprise. Then I turned to my main bully, pushed him out of the way, and hightailed it out of the locker room to find the teacher. That was it.

The level of physicality I used was appropriate. I might not have used the best techniques and I'm sure I did it much worse than when I would do the same techniques in my martial arts classes, but I can credit my martial arts training for the mentality of feeling confident and prepared to handle myself. I could ignore the constant teasing for a long time, but I drew the line at anything physical and knew that they did not have the right to lay a hand on me. I followed up by finding a proper authority (in this case the gym teacher), and that was the end of bullying for me. I never had another encounter again.

In a school situation, we're not teaching kids to respond to bullies by hitting them in the face or kicking them. We're definitely teaching a long-term solution. We're teaching your child how to avoid being an easy target, or better yet, how to avoid being any target at all. If you've got that covered, then having the physical martial arts techniques there to back you up only makes you feel more empowered. I think that knowing martial arts techniques is similar to having a fire extinguisher. It's important to have and makes you feel safe and hopefully you never have to actually use it.

CHAPTER 3:

KID POWER AND SUCCESS

The process of how to create a better kid and how to create empowerment is broken down into four steps.

Step One: Attitude

Attitude is a way of thinking about someone or something that affects your behavior and helps to make you who you are. No matter what people say or do to you, you decide how you will react. Attitude drives effort, and the more effort you give, the more you achieve. Major universities have found that people who succeed in life won't always have the best grades but are those who "out-try" everybody else. A positive attitude paired with a strong effort leads to greater achievement. Life is a contest with yourself to be a better you than you were yesterday. Everything is a learning opportunity if you take it. We're simply not always going to be the best. There is only one first-place prize awarded. There may be only one captain of the team, but just because it's not you doesn't mean that you won't make the effort to improve. Your attitude really can determine how successful you will be. So how can you have a good attitude? Your goal should always be to try your best, have fun when you attempt something new, and constantly strive to get better.

The lesson that I took away after being bullied in the seventh grade was that I wanted to learn how to play sports better. I wasn't an athletic kid growing up, but I think martial arts gave me the physical abilities, the agility, the flexibility, and the confidence to try more sports. Now as an adult, I play pickup basketball games and try other new things, too. I have some fun with it! Not only that, but it's a great way to stay in shape and connect positively with my friends.

Step Two: Take Care of Yourself

With a good, physical workout at least three times a week, you develop stronger muscles, stronger bones, and a better-looking body. You will also find that you are more focused and have a better attitude. If you feel fit, then you look good, and you're also less likely to get sick. Fill your body with good food by eating healthy as often as you can, and that will help you become even stronger.

A lot of times, people are bullied simply because of the way they look, and of course, in our society, you can be the nicest person in the world, but if you look a certain way, people may tease you.

A growing concern in the world is "shaming," as in body shaming or fat shaming. There was an incident with a video of a young man who was a little overweight and he was dancing. One of the "popular" girls, who was recording him, talked on the video about how gross and fat and out of shape he was. The video went viral, and many people came to his defense. I think he ended up receiving gym memberships and other things for free. People wanted to help improve the quality of his life because they knew he was such a good person inside and they wanted him to feel better and look better on the outside. This example is not given to mean that it's okay to be superficial or to think that looks are everything. Remember that we will combine this with the other steps to foster an overall good feeling in order to make us less of a target for bullying. Ultimately, it doesn't matter what you look like as long as you feel confident in your own skin. Whether it's in school or out of school, the same thing holds true. If you feel good, you look good, and adding self-defense or martial arts workouts will help you learn how to protect yourself.

Be sure to plan on at least three workouts each week. Many people are out there working to help eliminate childhood obesity, which has become a huge problem in the United States in the last few years. There are many programs available for kids, such as the NFL's Play 60 campaign, which motivates kids to be active an hour a day.

Martial arts, in particular, can work for a lot of kids who aren't natural athletes. In martial arts, you're not letting down a team; you're not sitting on the bench having to watch; you don't have to disappoint anybody. You're there for you. You go on your own and move at your own pace. You don't have to keep up with anybody else, and you're not compared to anybody else. You are held to your own unique standard and always pushed a little outside of your comfort zone to show growth and improvement at every step. Martial arts is definitely a great way and a fun way to get your exercise because of its constant challenges and ever-evolving curriculum, which will take you a lifetime to master.

So, plan on at least three weekly workouts of some type. Be consistent and try not to miss any classes. Take care of yourself by eating healthy. Learn self-defense. These steps will make you less of a target for bullies. With a strong body and new confidence, you can eliminate fear from your life and be ready to achieve anything you want.

Step Three: Have a Team of Champion Friends

It's really important to pick good friends. Studies show that you typically are just like the five people you hang out with the most, so choose your friends wisely. Stay away from troublemakers or others who do bad things. Team up with your friends and become leaders, and only do things that will help all of you accomplish great things in your lives. Hang out with your team of champion friends, and work together to get smarter and healthier and have fun.

When I was growing up, I know for a fact that a couple of my friends were bullies who sometimes made wrong choices. A great example of this was one day in the summer when a group of my friends and I were hanging out at a playground at a middle school that was close to our neighborhood. Some of my buddies got this big idea—they wanted to climb the flagpole and steal the flag. Right off the bat, I told them, "Not a good idea." I convinced a few of them not to, but a couple more were just dead set on doing it. Half of the group left with me, and we went somewhere to do something else, but the other kids stayed. The police showed up. The kids didn't get in any real trouble because they were just 10 years old or so, but obviously, they didn't make the best choice. The fact that I was able to leave them behind because I knew they were a bad influence saved me from getting in trouble that day.

I can recall being in middle school when I had my first exposure to drugs. I found out a kid who I considered to be my friend was smoking pot. I ended up distancing myself from him because I knew I didn't want to be around that. I knew that it wouldn't make me better, and getting involved with him and that culture wouldn't improve my quality of life.

There were other instances when some of my friends made bad choices, but I could not involve myself in their activities. They were tough decisions, but ultimately, I know that I used sound judgment. Good people can get caught up with bad people and can end up ruining their lives. You should find a good core group of friends to associate with. Let their desirable qualities rub off on you. Think about the top five people with whom you are friends. Hopefully, they are on the right path, and you have yourself a good team, so stay with them.

Step Four: The Ladder of Success

Every day, you get chances to make a lot of decisions. Good decisions help you get closer to your goals, while bad decisions take you farther from your goals. Let us envision a ladder of success with all your goals and dreams at the top of it. Every time you make the right choice, you climb up the ladder faster and faster toward your goals. With the wrong choice, you drop down a step. Don't do something wrong just because it's fun. If you're not completely sure about a choice, ask a family member, a teacher, or a friend to help you. Using good judgment can contribute to your success. Success breeds confidence, which, in turn, breeds more confidence. At the end of every day, ask yourself, "How did I climb the ladder of success today? What did I do to set myself up for success?" There may be days or weeks that you work really hard without much to show for your efforts. But then you may follow that with a really productive, successful phase. It's important to make choices that will take you closer to your goals, and with hard work and correct choices, you can climb the ladder of success.

CHAPTER 4:

A PERSONAL EXAMPLE OF HOW MARTIAL ARTS CAN HELP

I'd like to share an email from the parents of one of my students. Her name is Avary. She's about 10 years old, and she does catalog modeling for popular mainstream stores. Avary is a very vocal young lady, with self-esteem through the roof. She's just a great girl. She's very tough. Right now, she's on the hunt for a sparring state champion title which shows her grit, determination, and intense focus over a long period of time, which isn't something you see everyday in a 10 year old.

Avary is one of those girls who could be an "alpha girl," who could have a lot of social influence and tease people if she wanted to. Instead, she's so sweet and down to earth.

Let me share this email from her parents:

> *I just wanted to reach out and acknowledge the value and important role your program*

has played in Avary's development. Your program helps to reinforce the discipline and leadership qualities we strive to nurture in Avary. I wanted to share two recent events with you where Avary exemplified great black belt and leadership qualities. On one occasion in school, Avary stood up for a friend who was being picked on by older students. While I believe most of it was in jest, it was nevertheless having a negative effect on that particular girl being singled out. The girls were hesitant to involve a teacher because they were concerned about the older girls getting into too much trouble. Avary was the only one of the classmates who was willing to approach the group of older girls and respectfully ask them to stop. In another instance, Avary stood up for a friend who was being picked on in a one-on-one situation. She was able to convince the other girl to stop picking on her friend. While we are very proud of Avary and want to recognize her for her actions, I also wanted to acknowledge the role your program plays in the development of your students.

— Justin and Jennifer, Avary's parents

That email pretty much sums up everything we talk about. The fact that she's been in martial arts for so long meant that she had the tools to approach these situations tactfully. She was able to confront these people without escalating the situation, and it was enough to get her friends out of trouble. I think Avary's approach is pretty typical of what we're trying to do. Not everyone knows how to do what she did—Avary is definitely a leader in that regard. She wanted to do something and acted on it, and having a background in martial arts gave her the tools to be able to act appropriately. We'll talk more about how to act in a situation if you feel you need to do something about a bully.

CHAPTER 5:

WHEN IS IT BULLYING?

The first thing to think about when you suspect that bullying may be taking place is whether or not it's actually bullying. What are some bullying scenarios you might encounter? What do bullies do?

- Bullies make fun of people through teasing, calling people names, or taunting.

- They may spread gossip or malicious rumors.

- They may leave people out of activities.

- Physical bullying includes hitting, punching, kicking, or destroying property.

- Cyber bullying is sending harassing emails, texts, or posting mean things on social websites or blogs.

Now that we know what bullying is, we can look for it when it happens—or know when it's not happening. Let's play "Is It Bullying?" For example, let's say Student A runs into Student B and Student B drops his or her books all over the floor. Is that bullying? Most kids will say, "Yes!"

to which I respond, "No, that's an accident." Let's take that same scenario but Student A does it again, the exact same incident, every day in a row for a week. Is that bullying now if it happens repeatedly? Yes, that's bullying. Look at another situation where Student A runs into Student B and knocks his or her books down on the floor and then kicks the books away from Student B. Is that bullying? Definitely. If it were an accident, Student A would either just keep going or say, "I'm sorry I ran into you; let me help you pick up your stuff." But if Student B drops his or her books and Student A kicks them away, the behavior exhibited by Student A is definitely malicious because our bully is going out of his or her way to make the other student feel bad or is putting himself or herself into a position of power over the other person.

In general, buzzwords like "bullying" tend to get erroneously thrown around, overused, and tagged onto many situations, some of which may not be applicable. It is often thought that if a child knocks another child down on the playground that the child must be a bully. Well, no, sometimes it can just be an accident. Maybe the kid just doesn't have good social graces. He or she knocks another kid down, and instead of saying, "Hey, I'm really sorry I knocked you down," he or she just goes, "Hey, watch out," and then runs away. That doesn't mean he or she is a bully. It just means he or she has bad manners or just doesn't understand how to handle that situation correctly. Remember that we learn how to live life through our experiences, both good and bad, and some children may not yet have learned how to deal with others in different circumstances. Come to think of it, there are adults who haven't figured that out yet either. Simply stated, not every mischievous act is an act of bullying.

CHAPTER 6:

WHERE DOES BULLYING HAPPEN?

Another key to avoiding bullying is to stay away from hotspots. Hotspots are the places where you're most likely to get bullied. You can ask both students and teachers, and you get the same answers—bullying takes place in the hallway, on the playground, in the bathroom, on the bus, at the bus stop, or anywhere there's little or no adult supervision. So, for example, if you're going down the hallway, keep your eyes up. If you see some kids that are bigger than you or who have bad reputations, stay away from them. If you can find another way to go, find another way around, and don't put yourself near them. Avoid places where the bully is likely to be. Not only that, but making eye contact is a great way to project confidence, making you less of a target.

When I was bullied, it happened in the locker room. I remember very vividly what occurred. The coach would go into his office where he had the windows covered with paper. Right away, that was a mistake because the coach would go in there and not be able to see what was happening in the locker room. That was all the incentive that the bully needed. He knew that he could strike and by the time the coach heard what was happening and came out of his office, the incident would be over. So the locker room, for me, was definitely a hotspot.

I talk to both students and parents about awareness and focus. Sometimes people aren't aware. They don't have that situational awareness or alertness. The alarm doesn't go off and they don't see any danger, and that's when they find themselves in trouble because something's going on. Then all of a sudden, they are wondering, "Wow, how did I get in this spot?" A lot of people get themselves in trouble just because they don't pay attention. Sometimes I'm scanning the street and I see up ahead that there are five or six rowdy guys who have liquor bottles in their hands and they're pushing and shoving each other and they're being loud and boisterous. What am I going to do? I'm going to cross the street and go to the other side. I'm not going to walk past them. It's not that I fear them, and it's not that I can't handle myself. It's just smart. It's that this is a potential hotspot, a combustible place where you know there might be trouble, so you avoid it.

In martial arts, we discuss the timeline of what will happen in your brain and in your gut when there's a conflict. First there is awareness.

Awareness is when you can see something brewing up ahead. Then there is alert, something is up. I compare this one to having a "Spidey sense" in that Spiderman can detect a threat even before he knows what it is exactly. Then there is alarm. Something has been triggered and you are in need of taking action. Finally there is post-conflict, where you evacuate the danger zone and follow up with an authority, as well as addressing any physical injuries.

In my situation, when I was bullied, there were many factors that led to it happening that I was not aware of when I was in seventh grade. Now I look back and think, "Man, this was like the perfect storm." The coach was in his office and couldn't see anything. My locker was right next to the locker where the bully was, so I couldn't go anywhere. I was right there in his view. In hindsight, there are things that I could have done differently. I could have moved lockers. I could have probably moved right by the office and that would have put me out of harm's way. Not to say that I still wouldn't have been picked on or that there wouldn't still be bullies, but the situation might have gone down much differently.

An incident occurred last year when my wife and I went to Disneyworld. It was around 9:30 in the evening. We were in line, and you know how long those lines can be. There was a family in front of us with a couple of small children. A group of about ten to twelve young people, probably high school kids, came up behind us in line. They were talking about being drunk. One kid might have been high, I don't know. They were swearing and pushing each other. I positioned myself so that I was between that group and my wife and the little kids that were in front of us. If something started happening, I wanted to make sure that everybody else was safe or that I would be the first line of defense if they decided to do something. Thankfully, everything was okay, but there were a couple of times when they shoved each other that they shoved into me. This is an example of what I mean by situational awareness.

CHAPTER 7:

TYPES OF BULLIES

We talked previously about how bullying comes in many forms. Listed next is a breakdown of several bully types.

The Jock Bully

The jock bully is somebody who picks on people because they're just not as good at playing sports as he or she is.

The Drug Bully

The drug bully is somebody who is involved with drugs, whether it's prescription narcotics or illegal drugs. When I was in high school, a popular drug was marijuana and it was everywhere. There were even kids who used to smoke it on the bus on the way to school. There was definitely peer pressure to try it, but if they offered it to me, I had the willpower to say no. I knew what it did, and I didn't want to get involved with it. The drug bully wants to get you to try drugs. This form of bullying is a little bit different from what we usually think of, but it's bullying nonetheless.

The Neighborhood Bully

Neighborhood bullies are also known as "area bullies." They think that their house, street, or neighborhood is better than yours. "My house is bigger than yours." "My neighborhood is more expensive than yours." You become a target because the bully thinks you "live on the wrong side of the tracks."

The In-Crowd Bully

This is the kind of bully you find in the movie *Mean Girls*. These would be people who think they're popular and have decided you're not, so it's popular kids versus the not-so-popular kids.

The Fashion Bully

The fashion bully is somebody who picks on you just because of the clothes you wear. You shouldn't be picked on if you can't afford hundred dollar jeans, but a bully might tease you because of your outfit since it makes him or her feel empowered over you.

The Music Bully

This type of bully uses another tactic to exploit differences in an attempt to start trouble. Maybe you listen to country music, or maybe you think country music is no good. Someone might say to you, "I listen to rap music, and I think that's better. Why do you listen to what you listen to?

You should listen to rap."

The Brain Bully

The brain bully is someone who is intelligent and teases those who are less intelligent. "You're not as smart as I am. I get better grades. I get this and that."

The Whiny Bully

There are times when kids whine to influence others and try to get their own way. When your mom says, "Clean your room," and you moan, "Oh, I don't want to. Do I have to?" you're trying to bully her into giving you what you want. Kids may complain about doing homework or chores, a form of bullying to get their parents to give in. At a certain age, I would put temper tantrums in this category as well.

The Prejudice Bully

The prejudice bully is someone who picks on people based on the color of their skin, their race, or their beliefs. This type of bully is very common throughout the world and is a great example of bullying behavior that is seldom outgrown and continues into adulthood, sometimes with scary ramifications.

The Older Grade Bully

The older grade bully is somebody who picks on people who are younger. For instance, when I was in seventh grade, the kid who bullied me was an eighth grader.

The Cyber Bully

Cyber bullying, one of the newest and most widespread types of bullying, uses electronic technology such as cell phones, computers, and tablets as well as communication tools including social media sites, text messages, chat, and websites. Examples include mean text messages or emails, rumors sent by email or posted on social networks, embarrassing pictures, and so on. Unlike other types of bullies, the cyber bully can act anonymously around the clock.

This account shows that people who are bullied in person are often cyberbullied as well:

> *I was bullied on the way home from school in 7th grade. Two girls followed me home one day and made fun of my family. They also took photos of me and posted them with nasty captions on social media. I talked to administration and told them about the situation. They talked to the two girls but they were not punished. Since I've started training in martial arts, I am now more confident in myself when I am around people who harass me. I am also more*

confident in my appearance now because of the fitness aspect that martial arts provides me.

— Janet, 14

CHAPTER 8:

DEFLECTING THE BULLY

Now we're going to talk about what to do if you're being bullied.

You know, the hardest thing to do when you're being threatened is *think*. The first thing you need to do is breathe and take a well-timed pause, or a well-timed breath. Something called "tactical breathing" is very important—practice breathing in through the nose and breathing out through the mouth.

Let's look at a scenario. Suppose somebody pushes you. What do you do? Many people would be quick to come right back and meet physical violence with physical violence. Instead, when that person pushes you, just take a quick, deep breath, clear your head, and then you can hopefully come up with a better tactic.

There's also verbal abuse. A lot of times, before a situation even gets physical, it starts with a verbal assault, with verbal goading. When somebody gives you an insult, again, just take a deep breath and choose an action that takes you in the direction you want to go rather than reacting emotionally and choosing to do something that will ultimately get you into trouble or escalate the situation. That's why you should just take a breath before you act or speak.

After you've taken a breath, you can choose an action. There are many actions or strategies that we can take when we're threatened, so if one doesn't work, we can go into another. It's just like sports: Let's say you're playing soccer and you have the defender in front of you. If you fake left and your defender moves left, you don't just stop and say, "Okay, here you go. Here's the ball." Instead, you have a strategy for that situation, and if that doesn't work, you try another one. If you fake left and your defender moves left, now you go right or you do a spin move. You keep trying different things. You try these things one after the other until you find something that works.

Strategies That Work

Find an authority.

The first strategy you might try is to walk away and go right to an authority. Whether it's a teacher, playground monitor, guidance counselor, or anyone else, just find someone who can help you.

Play a trick.

This strategy is sort of devious, but it works! If somebody wants to start something, you can pretend to sneeze or wipe your nose and go, "All right, I'm ready." Nobody's going to mess with you when you have stuff like that. You can also say, "Don't get any closer to me. I have a disease!" But that one can backfire if the bully decides to use it against you. All of a sudden, there might be a rumor going around the whole school that you have a disease. Finally, you can try to distract the bully. Point and say, "There's the teacher," or "Hey, look over there!" You have to use these tricks tactfully, but sometimes they work.

Walk away.

Another strategy is simply to walk away. Keep your eyes on the bully—you don't want to turn your back to somebody because that's dangerous—but if it's a very low-level threat and they're only trying to get a rise out of you, just walk away.

Use humor.

There may be times when somebody comes up and makes a joke at your expense. If you can laugh at yourself and roll with it, it makes you less of a target. It's hard for the bully to build on that, and it can defuse things.

Attract attention.

If the situation starts to feel really threatening, you can yell to attract attention. Start making some noise. There are video cameras everywhere now. There have been child abductions in which a stranger grabbed a child by the hand and just walked away. The kid didn't know that he or she should yell, stomp, kick, or scream. Those are great deterrents and can work against bullies, also. Nine times out of ten, yelling to attract attention is a great way to stop something.

Make friends.

Try to befriend the bully. If my bully had been a little bit nicer, I might have been able to say, "Hey, you're picking on me because I don't know how to play basketball, but you're really good, so why don't you help me?" Try reasoning with the bully. Try to find some connection between you, some common ground. A lot of times we hear stories on social media about bullies and their former victims reconnecting and finding that they have a lot in common. If it happens later, it can happen now, too. Reach out and see what happens.

Ignore the bully.

A lot of times, the bully is looking to get a rise out of somebody, and the person who gives them that satisfaction becomes more of a target. If you can ignore the bully and he or she doesn't have a reason to make you a target, you may avoid becoming a victim.

On the other hand, you can't ignore something forever. We had a student who started working with us at age 4, and he has been in our martial arts program for about six years now, so he's 10. He's the quietest kid you'll ever meet. I think in the six years that I've known him, he's probably spoken about ten paragraphs to me. Definitely a very quiet kid.

One day his dad came to me and said, "Hey, I just wanted to let you know that Walker got in trouble today." I responded, "Whoa, that is not like him at all! What happened?" The dad said that he disrupted a class. He yelled out in class and the teacher got him in trouble. I said, "Wait a minute. What's the real story?" The dad told me that the kid in the seat next to him had been picking on him for a couple of weeks, and finally, today, Walker had had enough, so he turned to the kid and said, "Stop doing that!" out loud in front of everybody. It was enough to stop the bully, but obviously, for the class disruption, he got in trouble.

When it was all hashed out, the dad was okay

with it. I was okay with it. Even the teacher ended up being okay with it because it was Walker standing up for himself. But he had ignored the bullying for so long that it wasn't working anymore. It put him over the edge, and he had had enough, enough for him to stand up for himself. So ignoring the bully is usually a good short-term solution, but it may not work over the long term, and it may require other strategies with it.

Reason with the bully.

A bully makes an outrageous statement, and you respond by saying, "Okay, whatever." You don't escalate the situation, you don't add more fuel to the fire, and you can squash it right there. If you're going to talk back, be sure that you have the right tools, the right words to say. If you get in a situation where you're verbally threatened, you can say, "So?" or "What does that mean?" This would not escalate things as much as "What are you going to do about it?" or "What are you looking at?" which could be interpreted as confrontational.

Find Someone to Talk To

It's also important to think the right things. If somebody starts picking on you, you might tend to start believing what he or she is saying. It's crucial to have a support system in place and to have the right friends and/or other people that you can talk to. Many times people just get caught up in their own heads because they feel that they have nobody to turn to. The situation gets worse if they don't have that interaction and they don't have somebody who can tell them, "Hey, it's okay," or, "Here's the outside view of what's really happening."

Often when you hear stories of kids who are depressed or suicidal, it's because they don't talk to anybody. A few weeks ago, I found out that one of my students was having suicidal thoughts. She's 14 years old and has a lot of social pressures and things going on that she doesn't talk to her parents about. She never talked to anyone about it at the martial arts school, and she couldn't talk to her peer group about it because they were the ones putting the pressure on her. They were trying to get her to act a certain way, dress a certain way, be a certain way, and she got it in her head that "man, maybe these guys are right." But you should never think that it's your fault that you're being bullied because there's something wrong with you. Talking to someone else can definitely help out.

So remember, if one strategy doesn't work, use

another one. And always, always follow it up by talking to someone about your experiences. Don't keep your feelings bottled up inside you. Talking to someone can help you feel less alone.

CHAPTER 9:

DON'T BE A TARGET

In order to keep someone from bullying you, you need to act like you're not a target or a kid that can be bullied.

Maintain a Proper Stance

Your stance is your posture or the way you stand. At our martial arts school, we practice good body posture, which means maintaining a strong physical stance. From day one in martial arts class, we talk about body posture, and the first lesson is always to stand up straight and tall. If you walk slumped down, with your shoulders hunched, it definitely makes you more of a target. If confronted by a bully, turn your body sideways, keep your shoulders back, chest out, and chin up. Don't get into a fighting stance, but definitely put yourself in a position where people obviously recognize that you're ready and alert. Part of this stance involves having your hands up, so if you have something in your hands, it goes back. For example, if you're holding books in your hands, you turn so that the books go behind you. If you have a book in your right hand, you should put your left side forward and put your right side back a little bit. That way, the book can't be knocked out of your hands or you can protect it or put it down quickly if you need to. Keep the hands open, as this signals "stop", "stay back," or "I don't want any trouble," whereas the body language of having your hands up in closed fists says, "Let's fight." Your hands don't have to do anything, but they can be ready to block, evade, intercept, or, if need be, strike.

Keep Your Distance

I cannot stress this one enough—keep distance between yourself and the potential bully. If someone is close enough to you, they could touch you, which would escalate things. If you are outside their danger zone, you can keep yourself a little bit safer. I do a drill in my martial arts classes where I walk around and have the kids stay away from me, just moving a little bit with their hands up in a good stance.

Put Up a Good Face

It's important to have the right face or expression when you're facing a potential bully. To keep someone from bullying you, you have to look like a kid who can defend himself or herself, so you need to practice a confident look. A confident look is a look of constant concentration where your eyebrows come down a little bit, and you keep your mouth tight. It's not an angry look because that could escalate the situation. An angry look could be construed as saying, "Okay, this kid's trying to take me on." Think about somebody like Ryan Howard—he comes up to the plate with the bases loaded, and he's got to hit a grand slam to win the game. What kind of look does he have on his face? When he's staring down that pitcher, what is he going to look like? Or take LeBron James. He has the ball in his hands with two seconds left in the game and his team is down by one—what kind of look does he have? You know he's focused. You know what he looks like. That's the kind of expression you want to have when someone comes up and starts saying something to you. You have to have that determined look, that look of concentration.

Make Eye Contact

Putting on a serious face and making eye contact make you look confident. Looking up, looking ahead, and making eye contact also help you to be aware of your surroundings so you can avoid trouble. If you have trouble making eye contact and you just can't meet the other person's eyes, look at the forehead or the cheek. This gives the illusion that you have made eye contact.

Project Confidence

We know that people judge us based on the way we look and on that crucial first impression. If you look and sound like a person who can't be bullied, you may avoid becoming the target of a bully. Confidence is a bully's biggest enemy. You don't necessarily have to be confident yet, but try to look on the outside like you are confident. The funny thing about acting confident is that if you act confident long enough, it starts to become who you are. Though developing true confidence can take a long time, making the effort can put you on the path to avoid being bullied. Statistics show that if an adult takes on a new skill and wants that skill to develop into a habit, it must be done for fourteen to twenty-one days. If you fake it that long, it becomes routine. Actual confidence comes through training and practice. Life skills take a lifetime to develop and reinforce, but you can "fake it 'til you make it."

Use a Commanding Tone of Voice

When you are in trouble, pay attention to how you talk. Don't say, "I'm a black belt. I can beat you up." That will only escalate the situation. Instead, say things like, "Leave me alone." "Stop." "That's enough." Remember that it's not only what you say but how you say it. These phrases are self-explanatory and get your point across. They verbalize your expectations. It's important to practice saying them with a confident tone versus a weak tone. A confident response will have people's ears perking up, and they will take you more seriously. On the other hand, if you say "Leave me alone" with a weak, low tone of voice and also exhibit poor body posture, you might as well not say anything at all because it really has no effect.

I tell people that when they talk, they should use their Superman voice along with the Superman body posture. Imagine the "S" on your chest and tough it out. Sound confident and look the aggressor in the eye or on the forehead. Having a strong vocal tone is something we work on in martial arts training. We always talk about communication skills—how to talk, how to speak up. It's a confidence issue.

Let's say a parent brings his or her child in to a martial arts class to build confidence. One of the main things we're going to work on is tone of voice. If a child can speak more confidently, he or she is going to feel more sure of himself or herself. By the same token, if a parent comes in with his or her child and they want to work on self-esteem issues, we start by talking about communicating. Someone with self-esteem issues probably doesn't speak very loudly or clearly or is unable to get his or her point across, so communication skills help build self-esteem. If a kid comes in for self-defense classes, we are going to address tone of voice and the way that the young person speaks. Again, it's how you get your point across and make yourself less of a target. It really doesn't matter what the issue is since these are all interconnected. We use the same remedies to correct the issue. In my martial arts classes, we do a lot of role-playing, and we talk about how to speak. If you're going to speak to a teacher, maybe about homework, what tone do you take in your voice? How do you talk to your parents? If they ask you to clean your room, how do you respond? What is the respectful way to answer? How do you address bullying with your parents, especially if someone is bullying you? We address all of these topics, not just from the perspective of what words to say but also what tone to use.

If you can learn to use a commanding tone of voice in one situation, it will carry over into other situations. That's why confidence and respect are such an important part of our martial arts training. If you have trouble talking to your mom about what you want for dinner, you're definitely going to have trouble responding to a bully when he or she starts verbally assaulting you. Everything is interconnected—what you say, your tone of voice, and how you present yourself.

Share Your Experiences

Bullying is an extremely personal issue that affects us all in different ways, but it's one that many of us have dealt with at some point in our lives. By sharing our stories, we are often able to gain better perspective about our own experiences and take solace in the fact that we aren't alone. If you can raise awareness about the situation, you know you don't have to fight your fight alone. Younger children should always speak to an adult. Parents, if you hear your child talk about another kid repeatedly in a way that induces fear, doubt, or uncertainty in your youngster, it's worth investigating to find out more about who this kid is and what he or she might be doing to your child.

Follow Up with an Adult

Always follow up a bullying incident by telling an adult, but be sure to know the difference between tattling and telling. Tattling is trying to get someone else in trouble or to get yourself some attention. Telling, on the other hand, is simply reporting what happened. Telling is getting protection for yourself or someone else if someone is doing something that isn't safe or is hurting others. When reporting, it's important to be specific. Instead of saying, "I saw John bullying Sally in the hallway," add as many specific details as you can. "John knocked Sally's books out of her hands and got his friends to laugh at her and call her names."

When you have all these details, the teacher or other authority figure is going to take you very seriously. It's not just a boy or girl "crying wolf." Say something like, "Hey, look. This is what happened. I went into the bathroom and three girls followed me in and they put me up against the wall and knocked my books out of my hands and threw one of my books in the toilet." Now, all of a sudden, the teacher knows what happened. She can say, "Okay, I have these three girls. This is who it was. This is the incident that happened, and there should be some physical evidence there. Is your book wet? Did this happen?" There's more to go on. If there are more specific details, it raises more alerts and puts more information out there so that you're able to come to a solution. This is what makes teaching your child awareness even more important. They shouldn't be so scared that they can't remember or feel as though they shouldn't speak up about certain situations. That holds true even outside of school if something has happened. The more facts you have, the easier it is for the authority figure, including the police if they become involved, to be able to help you and get things done in a timely fashion.

CHAPTER 10:

HOW TO HELP STOP BULLYING

Remember that people who are bullies end up having fewer friends, get in trouble more often at school, and get lower grades. You can be arrested for physically hurting someone, and there can be legal consequences for damages to someone or to their property. It's not cool to be a bully. If you're a person who likes to bully other people, try to stop. Statistics show that 60 percent of those characterized as "bullies" in grades six to nine had at least one criminal conviction by age 24.

Be a Defender

What can you do to help? Be a defender. Make a promise to help others who are being bullied. Here are some good words to live by:

I will not bully others.

I will try to help other kids who are being bullied.

I will try to include other kids who are being left out.

If I know another kid is being bullied, I will tell an adult.

Repeating these phrases makes it second nature and helps change the culture about bullying. It helps kids understand that there are actions they can take to stop bullying and to help kids who may be a target of bullies.

Many schools have adopted this culture around the country as well. Schools are changing their cultures in various ways to back up those words. For instance, kids can earn points, stickers, coupons, raffle tickets, and other types of rewards if they help kids who are being bullied. If you do something right, there is positive recognition.

There are different ways to encourage this positive behavior that didn't exist ten, fifteen, twenty years ago. Back then, if you stood up to somebody, nobody might ever know about it. If you're the hero and you help out and do things, but you don't get any credit or validity or reward, it doesn't really encourage that behavior. Without a reward, some kids may not do anything. There seems to be a paradigm shift with a lot of today's youth that makes it easier to stand up and help out their peers. Nowadays, a feel-good story of someone doing the right thing can go viral, and they can be recognized outside of their social circle or even beyond the walls of their school.

The Bully Circle

The bully circle identifies the many different roles being acted out when someone is being bullied. Within the bully circle, there's the bully and there's the victim. However, there are other roles that revolve around those two in any given bullying scenario. There are the bullies' backups, the people who encourage the bully. Then there are those who are neutral, those kids who see the incident or the situation going on but don't do anything about it. There are also kids who see the situation and feel bad and want to do something. They have the desire to be a hero or to be a defender, but they don't know what to do or may lack the confidence to actually help. Finally, you have people like Avary, mentioned in the story earlier, who now have the tools and know what to do. They have the confidence and actually spring into action. These kids are the defenders. They are being forged in martial arts schools around the country. This is happening with a paradigm shift in their schools, open communication with their parents, and the valuable physical and mental resources that a great martial arts program can provide.

It's my goal to make sure that everyone can be a defender and that everyone knows what to do. If someone is being bullied, chances are you don't want to go stand up for someone else. If you do, it may only make you a target as well, and if you're not prepared to do the right thing, the bully will have two targets or the situation may become worse, escalate, and may become harder to diffuse.

A great martial arts program should work on building your emotional quotient or EQ. Your emotional quotient plays a key role in productivity, performance, and self-satisfaction. People who have a higher emotional quotient are more confident, more capable, and earn greater respect from their peers. It also helps to keep you calm, focused, and able to adapt to the situation to avoid having panic set in. Using your high level of EQ, you will be more prepared if you see someone being bullied. A great strategy is to keep calm and just go up confidently to the victim, take him or her by the hand, and take him or her away from the situation. It's the same thing you would do in any type of super-emotional confrontation like this, such as a domestic violence incident. The best you can do is to remove yourself and the victim from it. There's so much emotion involved and so many different things going on that if you take yourself out of it, you can make better, clearer decisions. Move the victim away from the bully and give him or her words of encouragement and empowerment such as, "You don't deserve that treatment," or "I think you're a great person." That helps to empower the victim and takes away some of the power of the bully.

When you act positively in a situation like that,

it rallies the other kids who don't know what to do but want to help. Suddenly, you get more people involved. It takes the people who are neutral and makes them look at the situation again. Maybe they say, "Well, next time, I might do something about this." It takes the people who were backing the bully and makes them think twice. They may think, "Wow, I wasn't on the right side of this issue." It really does help to change mindsets if you do it the right way. The wrong way would be to come up next to the victim and say aggressively to the bully, "Leave him (or her) alone!" That escalates the situation by encouraging the bully—now he or she is getting exactly what he or she wants. And don't forget: always, always follow up with an adult after you've seen or been part of a bullying situation, especially if something upsets you or someone else emotionally.

Reach Out

Tell the kid who is doing the bullying to stop. Reach out in friendship or try to support the kid who is being bullied in some way. Use the strategies that we've discussed. Again, the more you can get involved with somebody who is a victim, the more you may impact his or her life. You never know. Just one positive word of encouragement can change someone's life. Tell someone, "Hey, I really appreciate your friendship," or, "Come on over here and be a part of what we're doing." You could really turn things around for someone.

At the end of the day, we're trying to help people respect each other. We show that respecting everybody and saying a kind word when it's called for can change the world. If our culture could be based on everybody being kind to one another, what a better place this world would be! Negativity comes out so easily and we see examples of that on the news every day. It's harder to come forth with something positive and to stand out positively in a noisy world.

One Black Belt at a Time

One of our mantras that we use in our martial arts school is:

We help change the world one black belt at a time.

Children who earned their black belt reported that they were far less fearful of being bullied. One explanation for this is the additional psychological benefits of earning a black belt in martial arts. Earning a black belt may create that feeling of self-confidence, thereby reducing the fear of being bullied. Keep in mind that this effect takes longer to manifest itself because reducing fear of being bullied or improving self-confidence is a longer-term process than awareness and physical safety training. Developing positive personal values take months, even years, and needs constant positive reinforcement. Beginner white belts with less experience will not feel the psychological effects of martial arts training as immediately as they may see results in other areas. Typically, a parent will bring a child to a martial arts school for one reason, but may see that another reason has become equally or even more valuable and more than enough to keep the child enrolled for many years.

Because of this, children who earn their black belt in martial arts are more likely to defend their friends from being bullied. This is not an unexpected result, as the fear factor drops while the confidence factor rises with increased amounts of training in martial arts. These characteristics take longer to solidify and therefore wouldn't be present in the beginning stages of a child's training in martial arts but rather would only appear as the student stayed with a regimented martial arts program that continued to reinforce confidence and safety issues.

When people train at an ATA martial arts school, they're armed with better respect, confidence, and physical skills. I know that every black belt leader I have in my martial arts school will go out into the world and do good things, and they may even be able to help make a positive impact in their immediate community.

Bullying and negative behavior will always be

around since, unfortunately, they are just part of human nature. However, I can train the kids who are in my school and under my tutelage. I can help prepare them for whatever might come their way. By creating a unified front with parents, teachers, guidance counselors, therapists, police departments, and the community, we can change the bullying culture and make the world a better place.

If you're moved to help stop bullying in your community, you may find that a martial arts program works for you. I can only speak about my martial arts program and my organization, the American Taekwondo Association (ATA). The benefits to being a part of the ATA are many. There is a consistent program being taught in over 1,500 schools worldwide. We have the backing of a large organization that is always on the cutting edge of martial arts training and technology, always seeking out the best educational material as well as the best practices and methods to disseminate the information to the schools. Also, because schools are individually owned and operated, they have the mom-and-pop feel and close-knit community vibe, so you're sure to create a good rapport with your ATA instructor. ATA Martial Arts schools have teamed up with Olweus Bully Education and Amber Alert safety training to provide a well-rounded curriculum with specialized training available uniquely to ATA Martial Arts instructors. It may not be replicated in other martial arts, kids' martial arts, or other Taekwondo programs. In the end, find a program that suits your needs, fits your philosophical and family-oriented goals, and that you feel comfortable with. Choose a martial arts program that highlights life skills and empowerment as much as traditional kicking and punching techniques. It is my hope that this book will provide insight into how martial arts training will help empower your child, educate parents and school administrators, and see that there is a measurable positive effect to staying with a martial arts program over the long-term.

You can contact me, Master Marc Jouan, at my school in the West Chester/Downingtown/ Exton, Pennsylvania area at:

www.ATAPennsylvania.com

Follow me on Instagram and Twitter.

Like and follow me on Facebook at Master Marc Jouan.

Also, you can find schools in your area that are members of the American Taekwondo Association at: www.ATAOnline.com

Additional resources that I use which are very helpful are:

Home of the Olweus Bullying Prevention Program, http://www.violencepreventionworks. org/public/index.page

Made in the USA
Lexington, KY
24 September 2018